Johan Garcia
Andres Ortiz

# Integrated system for the treatment of injuries or trauma

Johan Garcia
Andres Ortiz

# Integrated system for the treatment of injuries or trauma

## Practical exercises of the ulnar-radial joint by means of a system

ScienciaScripts

**Imprint**
Any brand names and product names mentioned in this book are subject to trademark, brand or patent protection and are trademarks or registered trademarks of their respective holders. The use of brand names, product names, common names, trade names, product descriptions etc. even without a particular marking in this work is in no way to be construed to mean that such names may be regarded as unrestricted in respect of trademark and brand protection legislation and could thus be used by anyone.

Cover image: www.ingimage.com

This book is a translation from the original published under ISBN 978-620-0-42695-6.

Publisher:
Sciencia Scripts
is a trademark of
International Book Market Service Ltd., member of OmniScriptum Publishing Group
17 Meldrum Street, Beau Bassin 71504, Mauritius
Printed at: see last page
**ISBN: 978-620-2-82398-2**

# Dedication

*To my parents... for their unconditional support throughout my training period in the career.*

*To the teachers who contributed with teachings in this training period.*

*Concern for man and his destiny must always be the primary interest of all technical effort. Never forget this between your diagrams and equations.*

**Albert Einstein**

# Acknowledgements

I want to express my gratitude to my parents who have supported me throughout my career and have been there to give me strength in adverse times.

To my teachers who, through their teachings, have contributed to my ethical and professional formation, challenging me in my daily life during this formation process.

# Summary

This document describes the realization of a project aimed at the treatment of injuries from fractures, Parkinson's disease, carpal tunnel among other syndromes in the ulnar-radial joint that affects the lives of many people today.

For this purpose, the already existing device called "Metacarpal rehabilitation system by means of a maze" was taken, which is part of the academic process in technology, where a network is integrated that includes the physical therapist as a central node with the patients he manages, where the physical therapist's device acts as a server team and will be in charge of taking the data measured from his patients and generating graphs that show the progress of the patient being treated, comparing your measured data with data taken from a person without the syndrome or injury being treated, for this purpose the "client" device or patient device will be integrated with 14 levels that treat the above mentioned syndromes, additionally the physical therapist will have an application with network connection where he will be notified every time a rehabilitation session is performed.

**Keywords:** database, data, injuries, Network, rehabilitation, trauma.

# Content

# List of symbols and abbreviations

**NM-** Middle Nerve
**STC-** Carpal Tunnel Syndrome
**FDR-** Distal Radius Fractures
**SMS-** Short Message Service
**MMS-** Multimedia Messaging Services

# Introduction

Around the arrival of the second millennium there has been a massive increase in technological equipment thanks to oil exploitation and the advances in programming that gave an exponential rise in the same, thanks to this and hand increased several types of problems in the health of users of these teams, among these is the problem of metacarpals.

Globally, physical therapy has played an important role in treating this problem before, during and after, however, it has become almost an obligation for most people to maintain a work pace closely related to the technologies that produce this disease and this makes the recovery is affected negatively.

In Colombia, carpal tunnel syndrome is a condition that is not commonly or adequately treated. People who are not ignorant of this condition treat their rehabilitation inadequately, making their progress little or not at all effective. The exercises that are recommended are monotonous and not very attractive to perform, and this leads to the implementation of injections or surgeries to release the nerve, which can bring about negative side effects [1]

In addition to this, some patients ignore this condition, making it worse every time they continue to carry out their routine activities; this is because their economic income and personal motivation are not in their best condition. For this reason, an integrated system is proposed between the device already made in the technology stage that takes data on time and distance traveled during navigation in a maze game (client equipment).

A server that will only be controlled by the physical therapist, both mounted on the raspberry pi development card and the physical therapist's cellular device. The physical therapist doctor's server device is the only one that has the power to delete any data from any patient and at the same time to manage all the data from all the patients linked to the network. This device was developed through the implementation of tools such as apache2, phpmyadmin and php.

The "client" device or patient device was developed using the Python programming language and has 14 levels of maze, each with a higher degree of difficulty, the sensor that takes the measurement of the patient's movement was developed using the mbed development card and its integrated accelerometer allowing navigation through the different levels of maze proposed for treatment, it should be noted that the device has its own database developed in sqlite3 that allows each patient to consult their data individually.

This prototype aims to help those people who for one reason or another are unable to perform the exercises correctly by providing an affordable integrated system that will eventually adapt to the needs of patients and adopt new technologies and ideals to perform a proper rehabilitation of the metacarpus.

# Chapter 1: Problematization

Regularly in large industries, workers who manage the company's processes are tied to spending a large part of their working day behind a computer, which results in a silent condition that attacks the ulnar-radius joint and affects the health of the workers, better known as **carpal tunnel syndrome**, From now on named **"STC"**, this syndrome can occur through bad posture or bad movement when using the mouse during the working day and is already considered an occupational disease in commerce by the social security, the entity recognizes that this condition is occurring in several sectors of industry where physical activities are performed [2]

In addition to the STC, the ulnar-radius joint has another enemy that is generated due to an accident that may have been had, where through a blow, it affects an injury to the joint, depriving the person in the performance of their daily activities, of course it is the **distal radius fractures from now** on named **"FDR",** which occurs when the radius area near the wrist is broken in the forearm. [3]

## 1.1. Causes of carpal tunnel syndrome

Within the area of the wrist in the forearm, there is a nerve called the "Medial Nerve" which will be called from now on **"NM"** and has a space right in the central area of the forearm, if this space is reduced it immediately traps the NM producing pain and inflammation in this area, there are several ways that this event occurs, among which the most important are

1)      **Idiopathic Cause:** With several known possible causes, but in the specific case being studied, the specific cause is unknown, because none of the possible causes can be demonstrated.

2)    **Trauma or Micro-trauma: It** deals with occupations or activities that have repetitive movements, badly healed fractures, calluses among others.

3)    **Inflammatory Arthritis: Inflammatory arthritis** is a group of diseases that includes rheumatoid arthritis, ankylosing spondylitis, psoriatic arthritis and other spondylitis arthritis where the immune system that fights infection begins to attack the joints, producing inflammation. [4]

4)    **Pregnancy:** Some hormones during pregnancy can produce CTS.

5)    **Infections:** External virus attacking the joints.

6)    **Contraception:** Contraceptives, like pregnancy, produce hormones that affect the ulnar-radial joint. [5]


## 1.2. Current Ways to Treat Carpal Tunnel

The STC is considered an occupational disease that affects mostly women, this is due to local, regional or systematic causes, when you proceed to investigate and take action against the syndrome patients have several doubts about their treatment, so they turn to a physical therapist who through examinations determine the current condition of the patient and proceed to take actions which are:


-    **Pharmacological:** It is the procedure that is performed through medication that prevents inflammation of the central area of the forearm and relieves pain produced in the NM.

-    **Physiotherapeutic:** It is the way where through specific exercises, it is tried to free the NM of the central zone of the forearm, this way is the one that is approached in this work for the treatment of the carpal tunnel, at the present time devices have been developed that help the treatment of the carpal tunnel among which they stand out:

**a)** **Strength meter:** It is a device that stimulates the wrist area and replaces rehabilitation therapies, this device was made by the student Luisa Fernanda Morales at the National University of Colombia headquarters Manizales and aims to ask the patient to press a rubber ball for 30 seconds and through a force sensor records the force exerted on a multimeter in a range of 0 to 7 volts where each voltage is equivalent to a specific force in a range of 0 to 1 kg (kilogram) this device can be seen in Fig 1. [6]

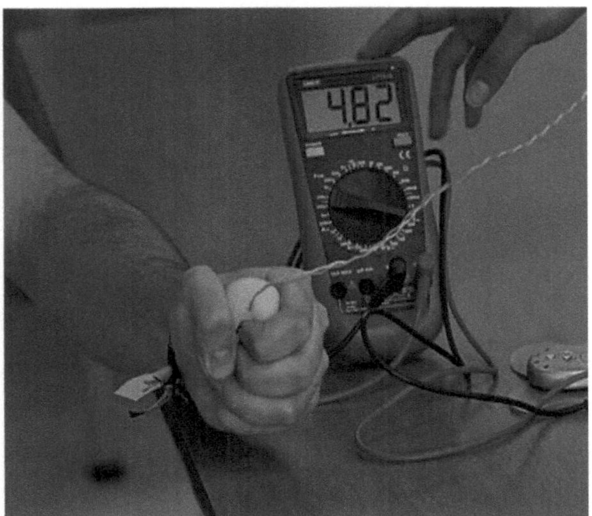

**Fig 1. Force meter**

**b)** **Wristbands:** Wristbands are a more focused way to prevent carpal tunnel where they act as a wrist positioning corrector, also help to relax the joint and keep the NM in a proper location, these can be seen in Fig 2. [7]

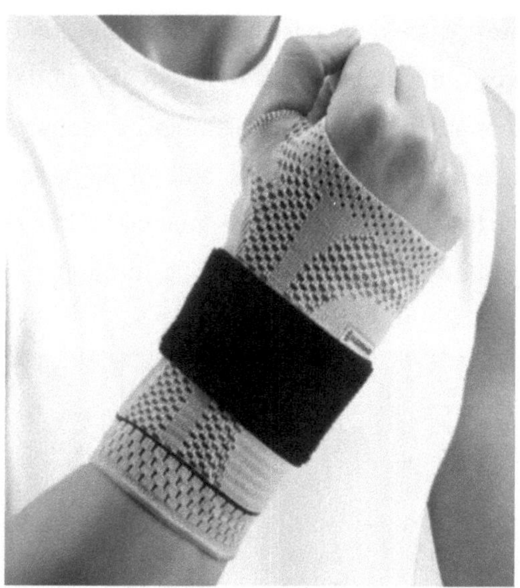

**Fig 2. Wristbands**

- **Surgical:** It is the procedure that is approached in the cases where the two previous methods do not have effect, it consists of making an incision in the area of the ulnar-radius joint accessing the central area of the forearm and releasing the NM manually. [8]


## 1.3. Current Fracture Treatment

Just as with STC, FDRs are treated by means of surgical procedures, where the most difficult thing is to recover the normal curvatures of the radius that has curved and straight places in its physiognomy. These procedures vary according to the affectation that was generated after the deformation suffered in the joint where mainly the curvature of the bone is affected, the normal length of the bone, the rotational axis and the relation with the normal touch. [9]

## 1.4. Comparison between devices

From sections 1.2 and 1.3 it is possible to observe the ways of treatment to the ulnar-radial joint, where their physiotherapeutic ways are suitable, nevertheless they lack interactivity that motivates the patient to carry out the corresponding therapies, giving rise to an abandonment of the therapies and contributing to the aggravation of the syndrome, additionally it lacks a pursuit on the part of a physiotherapist doctor who advises the patient in his rehabilitation, From the above, this work proposes a means that integrates the adequate and interactive way of performing exercises and having a constant follow up of the physical therapist in the prevention as well as in the treatment itself of the STC and FDR, this also helps the physical therapist to perform balances and studies of his patients with the purpose of innovating the device and treatments for the patients.


## 1.5. Objectives

### 1.5.1. General Objective

To design an integrated device with a network and multilevel designed for muscular dystrophy, metacarpal tunnel or fractures in the ulnar-radius joint, capable of informing in an accurate and timely manner the data stored in each interactive session to the rehabilitation professional and that he can establish daily sessions for the patient's improvement.


### 1.5.2. Specific Objectives

1)    To design and implement a server with an administrator profile for the rehabilitation professional capable of immediately reporting the data stored after each session so that he or she can determine the patient's evolution and recommend the corresponding number of sessions.

2)     To design multilevels with interactive interfaces in Python with raspberry pi of adduction, abduction, flexion and reflection (right, left, up and down) with a patient profile, which allows you to adapt to the system, perform repetitive sessions, each with a greater degree of difficulty and generate stretching of the carpals and the ulnar-radius joint, thus evaluating the improvement in your condition in each session depending on the injury you suffer.

3)     Design and implement an application through MIT's inventor app, for a cellular device with network connection capable of notifying the stored data to the rehabilitation professional.

4)     Generate with the device a monthly report for the patient and the physical therapy professional where it shows a degree of progress in rehabilitation.

## 1.6. Justification

The starting point is to take the device developed in the technology stage, which has only a database and a single level of treatment, it is expected to create a network and implement it in low-income patients who do not have an aid to treat their injury, trauma or motor shortage in a nonprofit way initially, until a detailed study of the impact on a sector of the population suffering from these traumas. Solving the above described in the problematization, through a private network capable of taking the data in the session and transmitting them to a server which will receive them and make possible their reading in a simple way and whose access and visualization will only have the professional in the rehabilitation, besides it is intended to add levels that will help to a better interaction between the device and the patient.

# Chapter 2: Aspects to take into account for the development of the system

In the foreground what must be taken into account for the realization of devices or systems that have a database is a flowchart that reflects the logic and processing in which the data recorded with the device will be affected, this will give the author an overview of the skeleton of the system and will help in the design of the entire device, The first thing to take into account is that the device in which you will be working only has a simple database for a single level of rehabilitation and this can only be consulted from the device itself, so by adding multilevel will change the current structure adapted to these multilevel.

It should also be taken into account that a network will be designed and integrated with the physiotherapist, in this may occur that a data is not sent in the right way, not achieved all levels making the session incomplete and not have real data, thus having a failure in the data for the professional and not achieve the objective of improvement in patients.

## 2.1. Adaptability to Multi-Levels

Something that was discussed in chapter 1 was the advantages and disadvantages of current devices in rehabilitation both of STC and FDR, in the disadvantages the author talks about the little incentive that they generate for a person in the process of rehabilitation.

### 2.1.1. Adaptability of Multilevels to patients

The first thing to consider is the number of sessions suitable for this process, in an article by Vitonica a website for physical activities in people Miguel Angel Lopez Pareja mentions that sessions in a rehabilitation should be given in multiples of 5 [10]The author chooses 10 sessions because prolonging too much a rehabilitation would do precisely what is intended to avoid and is the abandonment of the process without being completely recovered or fully recovered, to this the author also takes into account that for people who start using this device will be difficult in terms of adaptability and use of the device so it is added 4 levels each with a different movement (left, right, up and down), this ensures easy learning to use the device and a total of 14 levels to be developed for each session.

## 2.1.2. Adaptability of Multilevels to the Network

For this part the author took into account the way of sending data, where the first thing to consider is where to send the census data, this arises the need to design and implement a server which receives and stores all data that comes to it, you must designate a team to replace this role, the author chooses to use the card raspberry pi because of its easy accessibility in the market in addition to providing the necessary tools in a mini computer for this need.

As for the way of sending data, it was determined to send these via web since this project is being implemented for the communication of physical therapists and patients over long distances, the raspberry pi has the Python programming language where it includes an ideal library for HTTP requests that translates the processes of Python programming language and leads to requests by methods of GET and POST HTML programming language also stands out for its ease of use in this case only requires the destination URL in later chapters will be obtained and explained its operation [11]. The main thing to consider when sending data is whether it is better to send a data packet with all the sessions or to send data for each level that the patient performs. To determine this, the author took into account the use of the urllib2 Python library where two types of data are generated for each level (Time and Distance censored), Taking into account this, if all the data were sent in a single packet, there would be difficulties in data traffic as there could be collisions between them and poor reception due to the amount of data.

## 2.2. Parameters to take into account from the Database

As mentioned in the previous subchapter, the author will use Python urllib2 to send the Time and Distance data recorded at each level that the patient performs; And the device on which the starting point will be made has a local database developed in sqlite3 that does not have all the tools to be the database of a network like the one being designed, it must be migrated to another alternative, the author chooses MYSQL for its great output and tools that supply what is requested by the project and has the adaptability with the programming language of PHP for the reception and storage of data via web, Now, for the design of this database, the first thing that the author took into account is the amount of data that will be stored in addition to those already mentioned (Time and Distance). The first field that every database that associates a relational data table must have is the field of the key or primary key where its function is to list the data that is being entered. [12]The second field to take into account is the patient's identification number, which will allow the physical therapist to search individually for the data of one of his patients and to generate reports of his evolution. The third field is the patient's name, which will indicate to the physical therapist whose data the report is being generated, The fourth field is the level that the patient performed that will help in the reports to observe the evolution of the patient with respect to data taken from a person without the STC and without FDR and the fifth field is the date of performance of each session that will indicate to the physical therapist if the data taken was performed accorcing to the times he established, for all the above, a total of 7 columns were set to provide the physical therapist with the necessary data to treat the STC and the FDR in his patients.

## 2.3. Process logic to implement

Because the use of the device on which the starting point will be made will be modified in a great way, it is necessary to establish the logical process on which the system that the author will develop will be governed, this will serve to observe faults that can be presented during the development of the same one, so the author will have the possibility of making the due corrections that are believed pertinent and taking into account what has been raised in this chapter 2, the author designs the flow chart that is observed in Fig 3.

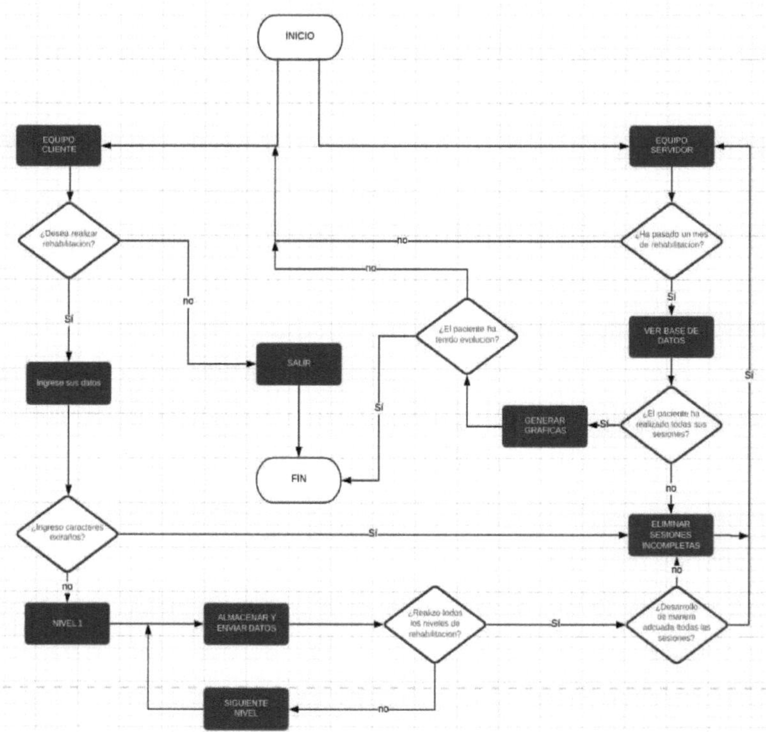


**Fig 3. Flow chart in the system process**

As can be seen in Fig 3, the process starts in two ways from the server device (the physical therapist's perspective) or from the client device (the patient's perspective) where in both cases it will lead to the patient generating the rehabilitation process in the designed multilevels where from the confirmation of the data it will arrive to store it in the server equipment in an amount of time that will be determined by the physical therapist.

## 2.4. Materials for the realization of the system

As a last measure for the realization of the system are materials to be used for development which can be seen in table 1.

**Table 1**:    Materials and Tools for the realization of the project.

| Materials | Software and function | |
| --- | --- | --- |
| | software or language | function |
| Raspberry pi 2 (Server Equipment) | Python | It is the main language on which the server is programmed and plays the role of consulting, processing and displaying the data of each patient |
| | PHP | its function is to receive the data that arrive via web from the client teams |
| | MYSQL | its function is to store and deliver the data requested |
| | PhpmyAdmin | its function is to administer the MYSQL database under an administrator profile |
| | Apache2 | Its function is to turn the computer into a server and make it accessible on a web level |

| Raspberry pi 3 (Customer Equipment) | Python | Its function is to take the data from the sensor, produce its census data, store its own data and send the data via web to the server equipment |
| --- | --- | --- |
| Mbed KL25Z | C | Its function is to census motion data by means of an accelerometer |
| PC or video beam monitors | | Its function is to serve as a means of visualizing the processed data |
| Jumper Connectors | | They serve as a guiding medium between the census and processing devices |
| HDMI and HDMI-DVI connectors | | They serve as a guide to PC monitors |

As can be seen in Table 1, few materials are required to start up the system, where two raspberry pi will be needed to establish communication between them, an accelerometer sensor that is included in the MBED KL25Z development board, means to visualize the data and connectors between them.

# Chapter 3: Compilation of all aspects and assembly of the integrated system

To start making the device the author took into account what was expressed in the previous chapters, where the first thing is the assembly of the server equipment, so an initial software update was made to the Client and Server equipment, then the installation of the software mentioned in Table 1 was made. Where an administrator profile is configured for the physical therapist with all privileges in MYSQL, then each subsystem is treated as described in Fig. 4

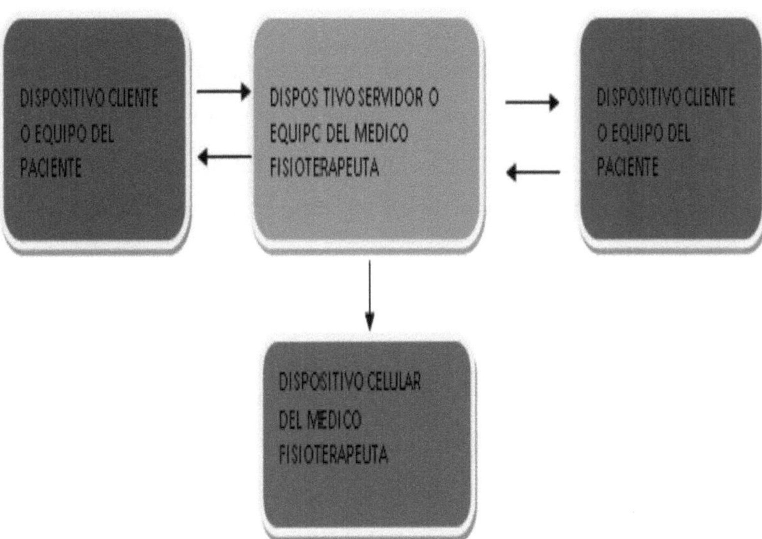


**Fig 4. Block diagram and project subsystems**

## 3.1. Serving Device or Physiotherapist's Equipment

This subsystem is made up of the server equipment or more explicitly the raspberry pi card which has the most important role and is to receive the data measured with the "client" device or patient's equipment, deliver this data to the physiotherapist whenever he requires it, either by the server device itself or by the application developed for the one discussed in subchapter 3.3, for the server device was made the installation of apache 2 whose function is to adapt the raspberry pi to be an open source server, where it works as a communication bridge between the raspberry pi and the different web servers that are in the global network internet, the programming language and tool MYSQL is where the table considered in subchapter 2.2 was created for all patients, this table includes fields like

- **Code:** It is the primary key of the database, whose function is to auto increment each time a data is entered
- **Identification:** It is the identification number that each patient has, this will be requested in all the devices "clients" or equipment of the patients, its function is to facilitate the search of some patient for the physiotherapist.
- **Name:** This is the identifier that will inform the doctor that the patient entered data into the database.
- **Distance:** This is one of the values measured on the "client" device or patient's equipment whose function is to inform the patient and physiotherapist, the patient's objective will be to lower the value of this data to generate progress in the treatment until a normal person value is achieved.
- **Time:** It is the other value measured in the "client" device or patient's equipment whose function is equal to the distance variable, the only difference being its unit of measurement.
- **Level:** This is the indicator that shows both the patient and the physiotherapist the difficulty of the environment through which the "client" team navigates.
- **Date:** It is the data that indicates the moment in which the treatment session is carried out, its function is to mark and identify the evolution of the patient.

Another application used by the author was phpmyadmin a powerful tool in database management and PHP programming language, whose function is to receive data coming via the web and enter it into the database created in MYSQL managed by phpmyadmin.

The interface of the server equipment to the physical therapist offers 4 sufficient options for the administration and management of the data that the "client" equipment or server equipment feeds, these options can be visualized in Fig 5.

**Fig 5. Main menu interface of the server computer.**

The options shown in Fig 5 are as follows

-       **Generate graphs:** This option allows you to generate two graphs (one to see the improvement in the distance item and the other to see the improvement in the time item) where each graph compares the census data with data from a person without the STC and without FDR as shown in Fig 6.

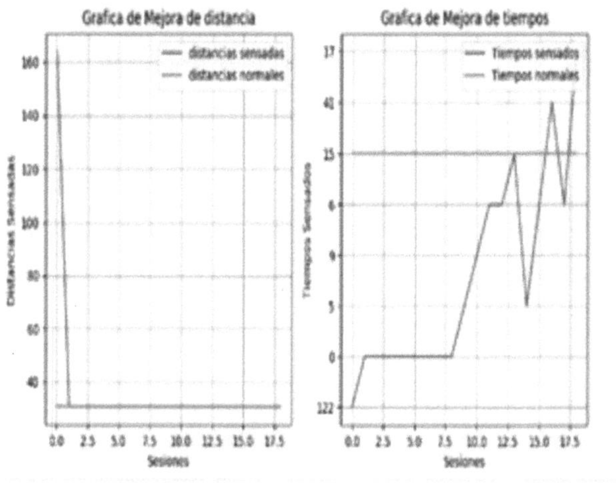


**Fig 6. Graphs generated from census data.**

Fig. 6 shows the graphs of the data taken in the "client" device and shown in the "server" device. These graphs are generated from the use of the matplotlib library that is compatible with Python scripts, the Python and IPython shells, the Jupyter [13]In addition to the previous consultation of the database where the number of sessions performed by the patient must be consulted, this number of sessions must be a natural number, otherwise the data collected by the "Customer" team is wrong and the records that were taken in a wrong way must be deleted, matplotlib is ideal to generate the processing and visualization of the census data compared to data taken from people without STC or FDR where the interpretation is that the blue curve resembles the orange curve, it should be noted that the data displayed in Fig 6 are data taken during testing in the development of the server equipment, so they do not correspond to data from a real patient; Initially, in order to generate the graphs, the device will previously request the data of the patient of interest, this request is shown in Fig 7 .

**Fig 7. Data request for the generation of the graphs of interest.**

In Fig. 7, two fields are required to generate graphs: the patient's ID number to filter the main database to obtain the requested data, and the number of sessions carried out. This data must be previously consulted in the option "See Complete Database and Last Data", and its function is to adapt the data to generate the graphs for a normal person.

-       **See Complete and Last Data Base:** This option allows the physical therapist to visualize the complete database of all his patients, where in a first instance he will request the data of a patient as in Fig 7, this in order to provide to process the data of the patient and determine the sessions that he has made to generate the graphs of his evolution, the visualization of the current database is shown in Annex B

In Annex B you can see in the final part, a message "the number of sessions are:", which tells us what value should be placed in the application shown in Fig 7, another functionality of the second option is to consult in a more graphic way the last data entered from the patient on which the data were entered when the consultation was made, where the date of entry is shown as we can see in Fig 8.

**Fig 8. Visualization of the last data entered in the database.**

What can be seen in Fig. 8 is the consultation in a graphic way about the last data entered by a specific patient, in order to generate a control over the patients by the physiotherapist.

-       **Delete Data:** This option will only be available to the server computer and will only be used by the physiotherapist, its function is very important because it will definitely delete the junk data that can be obtained during rehabilitation, initially requests the data of the value of the code to be deleted, where in the same way you must previously consult the entire database, this value will correspond to the value of the first column auto incremental, the request for such information can be seen in Fig 9.

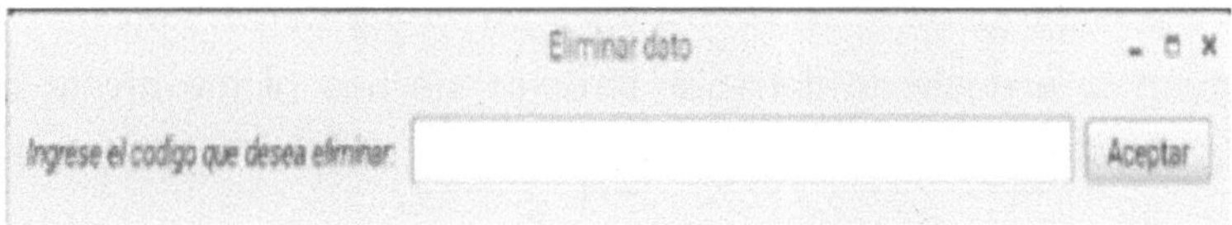


**Fig 9. Request for the code of the data to be deleted.**

During the tests carried out by the author, the data with code number 4 was eliminated, obtaining the message shown in Fig 10.

```
= RESTART: /home/pi/Desktop/ProyectoGradoIngenieriaJohan/ProgramaServidor.py =
Selecciono la opción 'Eliminar Date.'.
El dato ha sido eliminado.
```

**Fig 10. Message of confirmation of the elimination of the selected data.**

As shown in Fig 10, the deletion of the data is confirmed and corroborated by consulting the database.

-       **Exit:** This allows the physical therapist to leave the session in the system, showing as a final message what is shown in Fig 11.

```
= RESTART: /home/pi/Desktop/ProyectoGradoIngenieriaJohan/ProgramaServidor.py =
Selecciono la opción 'Salir.'.
 Gracias por utilizar este programa.
>>>
```

**Fig 11. Final message after using the application.**

In addition to the options developed in Python shown in this subchapter, the author developed a program for receiving data coming from patients via the web using the programming language of PHP and MYSQL. The language of PHP has a great advantage because it allows the interpretation of logic from several other programming languages, among which is MYSQL [14]The logic of the designed program is to receive the data through the POST method and assign them to a declared variable, through the use of the mysql_connect sentence you will have the use of MYSQL tools, that for this case it is only necessary the connection to the database mounted on the server and the use of the sentence "INSERT INTO" that allows to store the variables in the designed database, this program was located in the web output and input folder of the raspberry pi 2 and raspberry pi 3 whose location is "/var/www/html" the name of the program is **"indexphp.php"**.

Similarly, in order for the physical therapist's equipment to be a server equipment, the author assigned a fixed ipv4 to the device which was determined as "10.28.1.237", taking into account the url to which the data is sent:

<u>http://10.28.1.237/indexphp.php</u>

- **http://**: Extension of the Hypertext Transfer Protocol "HTTP".
- **10.28.1.237**: IPV4 assigned to the raspberry or the device being used.
- **indexphp.php:** Program designed for the reception and storage of data via web.

For the management of the database through phpmyadmin with the administrator profile, during its installation was requested the configuration of a profile where you add or remove the privileges that the profile will have, for this case was left all management privileges to the profile of the physiotherapist, this installation and management program is under the extension **"phpmyadmin"**, this program is by default in the web input and output folder of the raspberry pi **"/var/www/html"**, **so** like the data reception program is with the url:

<u>http://10.28.1.237/phpmyadmin</u>

This url is indispensable for the management of the database and can only be manipulated by the physical therapist. It is used for the development of the mobile application for the physical therapist that will be explained and discussed in subchapter 3.3

## 3.2. Client device or patient device

The "client" device consists of two development cards known as the raspberry pi and the mbed KL25Z, where the function of the mbed is to census the patient's movement by using the accelerometer incorporated in the card, the function of the raspberry pi is a little more complex since it takes the censored data and processes it to generate the displacement of a cursor in several maze interfaces. Initially, the generation of the different virtual environments with which the user or patient interacts takes place, the most important being the main menu shown in Fig 12.

**Fig 12. Main menu interface of the "Customer" equipment.**

As you can see in Fig 12, the device has 4 options as in the server equipment and each option has the same functionality as seen in subchapter 3.1 but the option **"Play and Exercise" is** added. This option allows us to enter the 14 different levels which the first 4 levels have the mission of teaching and adapting the patient to the use of the device in addition to generating stretching of the ulnar-radial joint helping patients with STC to a greater extent. The following 10 levels are focused on changing the stretching and mobility in the area of the ulnar-radial joint, thus providing the mobility and results expected in the rehabilitation and use of this project.

It can be seen in Annex C that each level has a higher degree of difficulty as you go up the levels to level 14 where all movements are used continuously, just as in the server computer before addressing these 14 levels we the program will request two vital fields for the management of data requested and recorded during the use of the device as shown in Fig 13.

**Fig 13. Request for patient data.**

Fig. 13 shows the application for the patient's ID number and name, the data entered in these fields will be those entered in the general database and the name entered will be the one sent to the mobile application developed to notify the physical therapist, in general terms the data recorded will be assigned to the patient who registers in these two fields.

To send the data via web the author uses the urllib2 library of Python, which handles the HTTP protocol and offers a friendly view, because the interface is graphical and does not have to understand the tedious code that this translates internally [15]The system simply takes the data supplied by Python, translates it into HTTP language and performs the file transfer using a string of characters called the WEB address or URL [16]. In this case the data is sent to the url http://10.28.1.237/indexphp.php explained in subchapter 3.1.

The client team can only perform queries from the internal database in sqlite3, whose data must match the main database. The option to delete the data is only available to the physical therapist, since he is the one who determines whether the data was taken correctly or not.

## 3.3. Physiotherapist's Cellular Device

In this part of the work is developed a mobile application that allows you to run queries of data stored in the general database, the physiotherapist should only have data service or wifi on your mobile device, this application is developed in the App Inventor 2 tool from MIT that is available online; The necessity to make this application is given through generating a way in which the doctor can make the consultation from a different place to the location of the server equipment, the mobile application must count on an easy interface to understand for the users, for such reason the interface is developed that is shown in Fig 14.

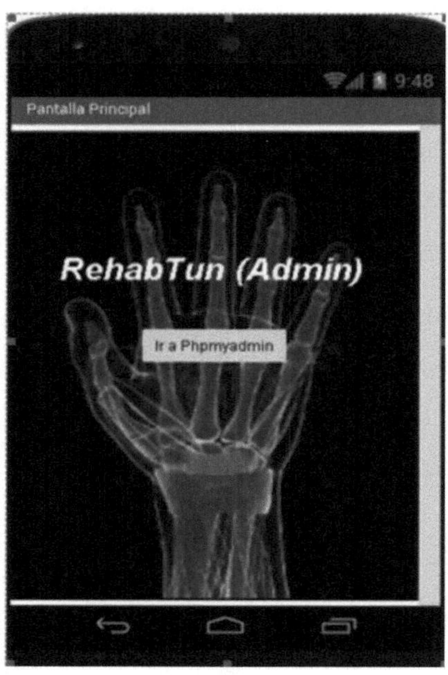



**Fig 14. Physiotherapist's mobile application interface**

As shown in Fig 14 the interface is very simple, it is named RehabTun and has a button that generates the connection to the network, where it will display a login screen, where the user and password are those configured during the installation process of phpmyadmin made in subchapter 3.1, this interface is shown in Fig 15.

**Fig 15. phpmyadmin login interface (administrator profile).**

When the user and password have been validated, it will display a list for the creation of new and current databases, this start and management interface is shown in Fig 16.

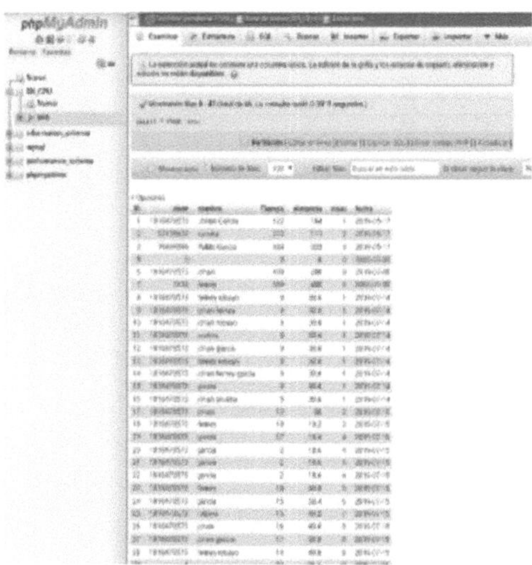

**Fig 16. phpmyadmin interface where the complete database table is shown.**

In Fig 16, in addition to the options mentioned, the interface shows the first part of the table that has been created and supplied by Python and the patients, in case the physical therapist wants to filter the general database and observe the data of a specific patient, he can do it from the toolbar shown in Fig 17.

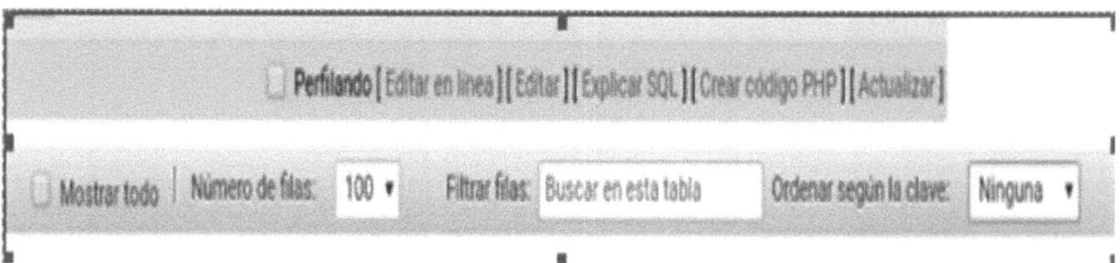



**Fig 17. Option bar for data management within the table.**

In order to send the notification to the physical therapist, the author used a Python library called Twilio, explicitly the author used the messaging tool, which facilitates the sending and reception of SMS and MMS messages, as well as the consultation of metadata on text messages [17]This is ideal for real-time notification to the physical therapist, where its use in the device is the inclusion of the library in the program of the client computer and when it makes the sending of data reaching the goal of each maze will trigger the use of a text message to the person who is registered in Twilio (physical therapist), Twllio provides a "Token" code for each user that will be validated in Twilio's main server for its use, so inside the client's program the login is done with this data to be able to use its functions for the functionality of the device, once this process is done the physical therapist will be notified with the message that appears in Fig 18.

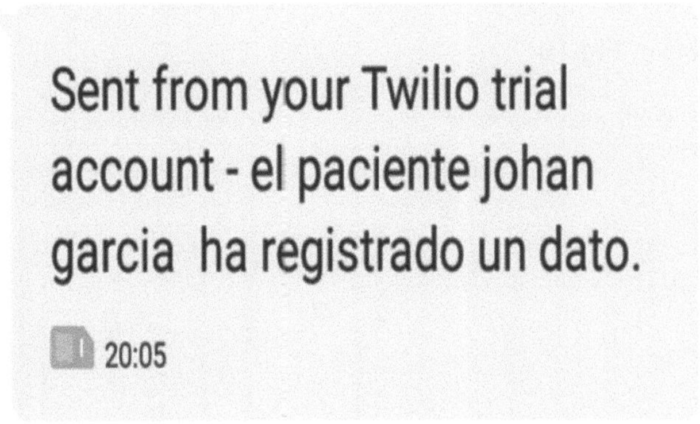

**Fig 18. Notification message to the physical therapist.**

The name shown in Fig 18, is the name that was registered in the data request interface of Fig 13, the notification to the mobile device of the physical therapist doctor takes approximately 3 to 5 seconds while performing the process explained above, according to th s the notification to the physical therapist doctor is in real time and he is permanently notified of the activities of his patients.

# Chapter 4: Results

For this chapter the author tests all the mentioned of the previous chapters in a person close to the author who will be called from this moment "the patient" who suffers from STC about 1 year ago, where in consultation with his physiotherapist doctor it was agreed to use the device for a period of 6 days, for each day to perform a physiotherapy session, the data taken during this period of time can be viewed in Annex A.

Initially, the patient found it difficult to adapt to the operation of the system, and this was reflected in his initial times, then on the second day as he adapted and as the days went by, he began to show work done and an improvement in his times as shown in Fig 19

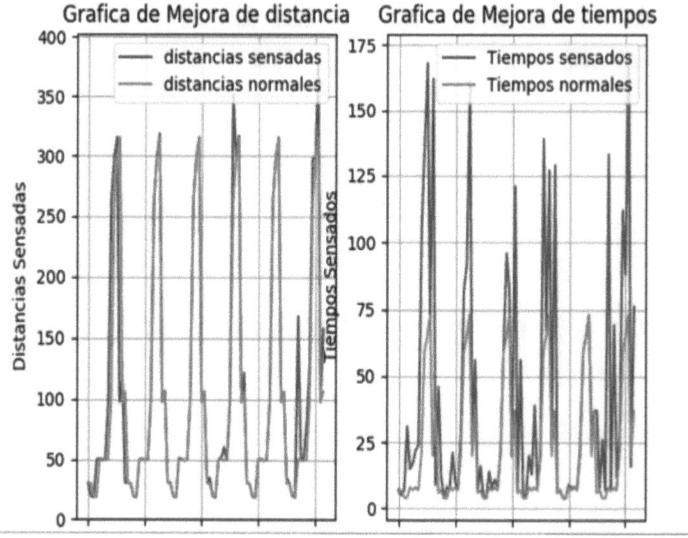



**Fig 19. Graphs with the test subject's results.**

Fig. 19 shows two graphs, each graph with two curves, one in blue and the other in orange, the orange curve reflects the normal pattern of distances and times in a person who does not have STC or FDR; the blue curve reflects the distances and times recorded in the patient, it should be noted that each wave or period of the graph reflects a physiotherapy session, for a total of 6 waves or periods in 6 days of sessions.

The graph of the distances does not have much relevance since it is done in the same route and there should not be a major difference, however, its function is to indicate to the physical therapist in which session and in what level of physical therapy there were complications and that he can take measures in the rehabilitation.

The graph of the times is in charge of showing the progress and the work done by the patient, where, as initially mentioned, the patient found it difficult to adapt to the device and thus his high times (see Fig 19). However, as the days go by, an improvement is noted and it can be observed that his times decrease, which shows that the device generates an adequate and interactive physical therapy work on the patient, where it is expected that after one month it will show more clearly its evolution and overcoming of this syndrome by expanding the central area of the forearm and releasing the NM, relieving pain and providing normal mobility in its ulnar-radius joint.

# Conclusions and recommendations

## Conclusions

- A functional network with multiple levels was achieved, capable of providing adequate treatment to people with syndromes or injuries in the ulnar-radial joint, providing constant communication with the physiotherapist and avoiding unnecessary displacements in patients with scarce resources.

- The improvement of the device was achieved in the technology stage that had difficulties in terms of the patient's adaptability to the device and its interactivity that motivates the patient to perform his rehabilitation sessions.

- The test subject showed promising results and a clear sample of work on the ulnar-radial joint that guarantees help to people suffering from these syndromes and injuries, thanks to the interactive way of carrying out the treatment and the multileveling with which it counts.

- The device eliminates the need to transport to the physical therapist, reducing costs and time for patients thanks to the network created with the various patients that the physical therapist has.

- It manages to create a device that provides relaxation and interactivity for workers in Colombia who suffer from carpal tunnel that are increasingly [18]This has generated an initiative to implement the device in different work environments.


## Recommendations

Within the Colombian industry, this type of device is not frequently implemented in STC or FDR, so a great impact is expected within the industry, which will lead to adaptations for the existing device that will include other types of ailments in different parts of the body. From a starting point, it is intended to improve aspects such as the distance range of the sensor to the raspberry that will allow greater comfort for patients who are undergoing rehabilitation.

# Annexes

## Appendix A: Table of patient data for 6 days

This annex is the data taken from a patient close to the author, where he carried out the rehabilitation sessions during 6 days obtaining the data presented below

| ID | ident | name | Time | distance | level | date |
|---|---|---|---|---|---|---|
| 50 | 1026579088 | Norbey Bustamante | 7 | 30 | 2 | 2019-08-13 |
| 51 | 1026579088 | Norbey Bustamante | 5 | 19.2 | 3 | 2019-08-13 |
| 52 | 1026579088 | Norbey Bustamante | 7 | 18.6 | 4 | 2019-08-13 |
| 53 | 1026579088 | Norbey Bustamante | 31 | 49.8 | 5 | 2019-08-13 |
| 54 | 1026579088 | Norbey Bustamante | 15 | 50.4 | 6 | 2019-08-13 |
| 55 | 1026579088 | Norbey Bustamante | 17 | 49.2 | 7 | 2019-08-13 |
| 56 | 1026579088 | Norbey Bustamante | 22 | 49.8 | 8 | 2019-08-13 |
| 57 | 1026579088 | Norbey Bustamante | 24 | 96.6 | 9 | 2019-08-13 |
| 58 | 1026579088 | Norbey Bustamante | 106 | 263.4 | 10 | 2019-08-13 |
| 59 | 1026579088 | Norbey Bustamante | 137 | 298.8 | 11 | 2019-08-13 |

| ID | ident | name | Time | distance | level | date |
| --- | --- | --- | --- | --- | --- | --- |
| 60 | 1026579088 | Norbey Bustamante | 168 | 315.6 | 12 | 2019-08-13 |
| 61 | 1026579088 | Norbey Bustamante | 68 | 97.8 | 13 | 2019-08-13 |
| 62 | 1026579088 | Norbey Bustamante | 162 | 116.4 | 14 | 2019-08-13 |
| 64 | 1026579088 | Norbey Bustamante | 9 | 30.6 | 1 | 2019-08-14 |
| 65 | 1026579088 | Norbey Bustamante | 46 | 30.6 | 1 | 2019-08-14 |
| 66 | 1026579088 | Norbey Bustamante | 12 | 30 | 2 | 2019-08-14 |
| 67 | 1026579088 | Norbey Bustamante | 4 | 19.2 | 3 | 2019-08-14 |
| 68 | 1026579088 | Norbey Bustamante | 8 | 18.6 | 4 | 2019-08-14 |
| 69 | 1026579088 | Norbey Bustamante | 8 | 49.8 | 5 | 2019-08-14 |
| 70 | 1026579088 | Norbey Bustamante | 21 | 50.4 | 6 | 2019-08-14 |
| 71 | 1026579088 | Norbey Bustamante | 10 | 49.2 | 7 | 2019-08-14 |
| 72 | 1026579088 | Norbey Bustamante | 7 | 49.8 | 8 | 2019-08-14 |
| 73 | 1026579088 | Norbey Bustamante | 28 | 96.6 | 9 | 2019-08-14 |

| ID | ident | name | Time | distance | level | date |
| --- | --- | --- | --- | --- | --- | --- |
| 74 | 1026579088 | Norbey Bustamante | 82 | 264 | 10 | 2019-08-14 |
| 75 | 1026579088 | Norbey Bustamante | 92 | 299.4 | 11 | 2019-08-14 |
| 76 | 1026579088 | Norbey Bustamante | 161 | 318.6 | 12 | 2019-08-14 |
| 77 | 1026579088 | Norbey Bustamante | 28 | 97.8 | 13 | 2019-08-14 |
| 78 | 1026579088 | Norbey Bustamante | 56 | 106.8 | 14 | 2019-08-14 |
| 79 | 1026579088 | Norbey Bustamante | 7 | 30.6 | 1 | 2019-08-15 |
| 80 | 1026579088 | Norbey Bustamante | 16 | 30.6 | 2 | 2019-08-15 |
| 81 | 1026579088 | Norbey Bustamante | 5 | 19.2 | 3 | 2019-08-15 |
| 82 | 1026579088 | Norbey Bustamante | 4 | 18.6 | 4 | 2019-08-15 |
| 83 | 1026579088 | Norbey Bustamante | 14 | 51 | 5 | 2019-08-15 |
| 84 | 1026579088 | Norbey Bustamante | 8 | 50.4 | 6 | 2019-08-15 |
| 85 | 1026579088 | Norbey Bustamante | 11 | 49.2 | 7 | 2019-08-15 |
| 86 | 1026579088 | Norbey Bustamante | 8 | 49.8 | 8 | 2019-08-15 |

| ID | ident | name | Time | distance | level | date |
| --- | --- | --- | --- | --- | --- | --- |
| 87 | 1026579088 | Norbey Bustamante | 22 | 97.8 | 9 | 2019-08-15 |
| 88 | 1026579088 | Norbey Bustamante | 62 | 264.6 | 10 | 2019-08-15 |
| 89 | 1026579088 | Norbey Bustamante | 96 | 298.8 | 11 | 2019-08-15 |
| 90 | 1026579088 | Norbey Bustamante | 82 | 315.6 | 12 | 2019-08-15 |
| 91 | 1026579088 | Norbey Bustamante | 20 | 97.8 | 13 | 2019-08-15 |
| 92 | 1026579088 | Norbey Bustamante | 121 | 106.2 | 14 | 2019-08-15 |
| 93 | 1026579088 | Norbey Bustamente | 7 | 30.6 | 1 | 2019-08-16 |
| 94 | 1026579088 | Norbey Bustamente | 56 | 34.8 | 2 | 2019-08-16 |
| 95 | 1026579088 | Norbey Bustamente | 5 | 19.2 | 3 | 2019-08-16 |
| 96 | 1026579088 | Norbey Bustamente | 5 | 18.6 | 4 | 2019-08-16 |
| 97 | 1026579088 | Norbey Bustamente | 20 | 49.8 | 5 | 2019-08-16 |
| 98 | 1026579088 | Norbey Bustamente | 13 | 51.6 | 6 | 2019-08-16 |
| 99 | 1026579088 | Norbey Bustamente | 39 | 60 | 7 | 2019-08-16 |

| ID | ident | name | Time | distance | level | date |
|---|---|---|---|---|---|---|
| 100 | 1026579088 | Norbey Bustamente | 9 | 49.8 | 8 | 2019-08-16 |
| 101 | 1026579088 | Norbey Bustamente | 20 | 96.6 | 9 | 2019-08-16 |
| 102 | 1026579088 | Norbey Bustamente | 139 | 352.2 | 10 | 2019-08-16 |
| 103 | 1026579088 | Norbey Bustamente | 67 | 299.4 | 11 | 2019-08-16 |
| 104 | 1026579088 | Norbey Bustamante | 127 | 316.8 | 12 | 2019-08-16 |
| 105 | 1026579088 | Norbey Bustamante | 23 | 97.8 | 13 | 2019-08-16 |
| 106 | 1026579088 | Norbey Bustamante | 129 | 121.8 | 14 | 2019-08-16 |
| 107 | 1026579088 | Norbey Bustamante | 6 | 30.6 | 1 | 2019-08-17 |
| 108 | 1026579088 | Norbey Bustamante | 7 | 30 | 2 | 2019-08-17 |
| 109 | 1026579088 | Norbey Bustamante | 4 | 19.2 | 3 | 2019-08-17 |
| 110 | 1026579088 | Norbey Bustamante | 4 | 18.6 | 4 | 2019-08-17 |
| 111 | 1026579088 | Norbey Bustamante | 9 | 49.8 | 5 | 2019-08-17 |
| 112 | 1026579088 | Norbey Bustamante | 8 | 50.4 | 6 | 2019-08-17 |

| ID | ident | name | Time | distance | level | date |
|---|---|---|---|---|---|---|
| 113 | 1026579088 | Norbey Bustamante | 8 | 49.2 | 7 | 2019-08-17 |
| 114 | 1026579088 | Norbey Bustamante | 8 | 49.8 | 8 | 2019-08-17 |
| 115 | 1026579088 | Norbey Bustamante | 23 | 96.6 | 9 | 2019-08-17 |
| 116 | 1026579088 | Norbey Bustamante | 59 | 263.4 | 10 | 2019-08-17 |
| 117 | 1026579088 | Norbey Bustamante | 65 | 298.8 | 11 | 2019-08-17 |
| 118 | 1026579088 | Norbey Bustamante | 73 | 315.6 | 12 | 2019-08-17 |
| 119 | 1026579088 | Norbey Bustamante | 31 | 97.8 | 13 | 2019-08-17 |
| 120 | 1026579088 | Norbey Bustamante | 37 | 106.2 | 14 | 2019-08-17 |
| 121 | 1026579088 | Norbey BUstamante | 37 | 35.4 | 1 | 2019-08-18 |
| 122 | 1026579088 | Norbey BUstamante | 8 | 30.6 | 2 | 2019-08-18 |
| 123 | 1026579088 | Norbey BUstamante | 26 | 20.4 | 3 | 2019-08-18 |
| 124 | 1026579088 | Norbey BUstamante | 7 | 18.6 | 4 | 2019-08-18 |
| 125 | 1026579088 | Norbey BUstamante | 133 | 168 | 5 | 2019-08-18 |

| ID | ident | name | Time | distance | level | date |
|---|---|---|---|---|---|---|
| 126 | 1026579088 | Norbey BUstamante | 7 | 50.4 | 6 | 2019-08-18 |
| 127 | 1026579088 | Norbey BUstamante | 69 | 51.6 | 7 | 2019-08-18 |
| 128 | 1026579088 | Norbey BUstamante | 12 | 76.2 | 8 | 2019-08-18 |
| 129 | 1026579088 | Norbey BUstamante | 27 | 128.4 | 9 | 2019-08-18 |
| 130 | 1026579088 | Norbey BUstamante | 112 | 297.6 | 10 | 2019-08-18 |
| 131 | 1026579088 | Norbey BUstamante | 88 | 299.4 | 11 | 2019-08-18 |
| 132 | 1026579088 | Norbey BUstamante | 171 | 384.6 | 12 | 2019-08-18 |
| 133 | 1026579088 | Norbey BUstamante | 16 | 97.8 | 13 | 2019-08-18 |
| 134 | 1026579088 | Norbey BUstamante | 76 | 157.8 | 14 | 2019-08-18 |

# Annex B: Complete Database

This Annex deals with the data stored in the database to date, in it you can find the data from Annex A of the patient who used the device for 6 days of rehabilitation.

| ID | ident | name | Time | distance | level | date |
|----|-------|------|------|----------|-------|------|
| 1 | 1018470573 | Johan Garcia | 122 | 164 | 1 | 2019-05-17 |
| 2 | 52125620 | sandra | 222 | 111 | 2 | 2019-05-17 |
| 3 | 79499599 | Pablo Garcia | 444 | 333 | 3 | 2019-05-17 |
| 6 | 1018470573 | johan | 400 | 200 | 8 | 2019-07-08 |
| 8 | 1018470573 | ferney robayo | 0 | 30.6 | 1 | 2019-07-14 |
| 9 | 1018470573 | johan ferney | 0 | 30.6 | 1 | 2019-07-14 |
| 10 | 1018470573 | johan robayo | 0 | 30.6 | 1 | 2019-07-14 |
| 11 | 1018470573 | andres | 0 | 30.6 | 1 | 2019-07-14 |
| 12 | 1018470573 | johan garcia | 0 | 30.6 | 1 | 2019-07-14 |
| 13 | 1018470573 | ferney robayo | 0 | 30.6 | 1 | 2019-07-14 |
| 14 | 1018470573 | johan ferney garcia | 0 | 30.6 | 1 | 2019-07-14 |
| 15 | 1018470573 | garcia | 0 | 30.6 | 1 | 2019-07-14 |
| 16 | 1018470573 | johan test | 5 | 30.6 | 1 | 2019-07-14 |
| 17 | 1018470573 | johan | 12 | 30 | 2 | 2019-07-15 |
| 18 | 1018470573 | ferney | 10 | 19.2 | 3 | 2019-07-15 |
| 19 | 1018470573 | garcia | 17 | 18.6 | 4 | 2019-07-15 |

| ID | ident | name | Time | distance | level | date |
|---|---|---|---|---|---|---|
| 20 | 1018470573 | garcia | 2 | 18.6 | 4 | 2019-07-15 |
| 21 | 1018470573 | garcia | 2 | 18.6 | 4 | 2019-07-15 |
| 22 | 1018470573 | garcia | 2 | 18.6 | 4 | 2019-07-15 |
| 23 | 1018470573 | ferney | 15 | 49.8 | 5 | 2019-07-15 |
| 24 | 1018470573 | garcia | 15 | 50.4 | 6 | 2019-07-15 |
| 25 | 1018470573 | robayo | 15 | 49.2 | 7 | 2019-07-15 |
| 26 | 1018470573 | johan | 16 | 49.8 | 8 | 2019-07-15 |
| 27 | 1018470573 | johan garcia | 17 | 49.8 | 8 | 2019-07-15 |
| 28 | 1018470573 | ferney robayo | 14 | 49.8 | 8 | 2019-07-15 |
| 32 | 1018470573 | ferney | 231 | 315.6 | 12 | 2019-07-16 |
| 35 | 1018470573 | johanMS | 9 | 30.6 | 1 | 2019-07-17 |
| 36 | 1018470573 | JohanSMS2 | 6 | 30.6 | 1 | 2019-07-17 |
| 37 | 1018470573 | johanSMS3 | 6 | 30.6 | 1 | 2019-07-17 |
| 38 | 1018470573 | johan | 15 | 30.6 | 1 | 2019-07-22 |
| 39 | 1018470573 | johan | 5 | 30.6 | 1 | 2019-07-22 |
| 40 | 1018470573 | johan | 6 | 30.6 | 1 | 2019-07-22 |
| 41 | 1018470573 | johan | 41 | 30.6 | 1 | 2019-07-23 |
| 42 | 1018470573 | johan | 6 | 30.6 | 1 | 2019-07-23 |
| 43 | 1018470573 | johan | 17 | 30.6 | 1 | 2019-07-31 |
| 44 | 1018470573 | johan | 27 | 30 | 2 | 2019-07-31 |

| ID | ident | name | Time | distance | level | date |
|---|---|---|---|---|---|---|
| 45 | 1018470573 | johan | 806 | 19.2 | 3 | 2019-07-31 |
| 46 | 1018470573 | johan garcia | 19 | 30.6 | 1 | 2019-08-12 |
| 47 | 1018470573 | johan garcia | 6 | 30.6 | 1 | 2019-08-12 |
| 50 | 1026579088 | Norbey Bustamante | 7 | 30 | 2 | 2019-08-13 |
| 51 | 1026579088 | Norbey Bustamante | 5 | 19.2 | 3 | 2019-08-13 |
| 52 | 1026579088 | Norbey Bustamante | 7 | 18.6 | 4 | 2019-08-13 |
| 53 | 1026579088 | Norbey Bustamante | 31 | 49.8 | 5 | 2019-08-13 |
| 54 | 1026579088 | Norbey Bustamante | 15 | 50.4 | 6 | 2019-08-13 |
| 55 | 1026579088 | Norbey Bustamante | 17 | 49.2 | 7 | 2019-08-13 |
| 56 | 1026579088 | Norbey Bustamante | 22 | 49.8 | 8 | 2019-08-13 |
| 57 | 1026579088 | Norbey Bustamante | 24 | 96.6 | 9 | 2019-08-13 |
| 58 | 1026579088 | Norbey Bustamante | 106 | 263.4 | 10 | 2019-08-13 |
| 59 | 1026579088 | Norbey Bustamante | 137 | 298.8 | 11 | 2019-08-13 |
| 60 | 1026579088 | Norbey Bustamante | 168 | 315.6 | 12 | 2019-08-13 |

| ID | ident | name | Time | distance | level | date |
|----|-------|------|------|----------|-------|------|
| 61 | 1026579088 | Norbey Bustamante | 68 | 97.8 | 13 | 2019-08-13 |
| 62 | 1026579088 | Norbey Bustamante | 162 | 116.4 | 14 | 2019-08-13 |
| 64 | 1026579088 | Norbey Bustamante | 9 | 30.6 | 1 | 2019-08-14 |
| 65 | 1026579088 | Norbey Bustamante | 46 | 30.6 | 1 | 2019-08-14 |
| 66 | 1026579088 | Norbey Bustamante | 12 | 30 | 2 | 2019-08-14 |
| 67 | 1026579088 | Norbey Bustamante | 4 | 19.2 | 3 | 2019-08-14 |
| 68 | 1026579088 | Norbey Bustamante | 8 | 18.6 | 4 | 2019-08-14 |
| 69 | 1026579088 | Norbey Bustamante | 8 | 49.8 | 5 | 2019-08-14 |
| 70 | 1026579088 | Norbey Bustamante | 21 | 50.4 | 6 | 2019-08-14 |
| 71 | 1026579088 | Norbey Bustamante | 10 | 49.2 | 7 | 2019-08-14 |
| 72 | 1026579088 | Norbey Bustamante | 7 | 49.8 | 8 | 2019-08-14 |
| 73 | 1026579088 | Norbey Bustamante | 28 | 96.6 | 9 | 2019-08-14 |
| 74 | 1026579088 | Norbey Bustamante | 82 | 264 | 10 | 2019-08-14 |
| 75 | 1026579088 | Norbey Bustamante | 92 | 299.4 | 11 | 2019-08-14 |

| ID | ident | name | Time | distance | level | date |
|---|---|---|---|---|---|---|
| 76 | 1026579088 | Norbey Bustamante | 161 | 318.6 | 12 | 2019-08-14 |
| 77 | 1026579088 | Norbey Bustamante | 28 | 97.8 | 13 | 2019-08-14 |
| 78 | 1026579088 | Norbey Bustamante | 56 | 106.8 | 14 | 2019-08-14 |
| 79 | 1026579088 | Norbey Bustamante | 7 | 30.6 | 1 | 2019-08-15 |
| 80 | 1026579088 | Norbey Bustamante | 16 | 30.6 | 2 | 2019-08-15 |
| 81 | 1026579088 | Norbey Bustamante | 5 | 19.2 | 3 | 2019-08-15 |
| 82 | 1026579088 | Norbey Bustamante | 4 | 18.6 | 4 | 2019-08-15 |
| 83 | 1026579088 | Norbey Bustamante | 14 | 51 | 5 | 2019-08-15 |
| 84 | 1026579088 | Norbey Bustamante | 8 | 50.4 | 6 | 2019-08-15 |
| 85 | 1026579088 | Norbey Bustamante | 11 | 49.2 | 7 | 2019-08-15 |
| 86 | 1026579088 | Norbey Bustamante | 8 | 49.8 | 8 | 2019-08-15 |
| 87 | 1026579088 | Norbey Bustamante | 22 | 97.8 | 9 | 2019-08-15 |
| 88 | 1026579088 | Norbey Bustamante | 62 | 264.6 | 10 | 2019-08-15 |

| ID | ident | name | Time | distance | level | date |
|---|---|---|---|---|---|---|
| 89 | 1026579088 | Norbey Bustamante | 96 | 298.8 | 11 | 2019-08-15 |
| 90 | 1026579088 | Norbey Bustamante | 82 | 315.6 | 12 | 2019-08-15 |
| 91 | 1026579088 | Norbey Bustamante | 20 | 97.8 | 13 | 2019-08-15 |
| 92 | 1026579088 | Norbey Bustamante | 121 | 106.2 | 14 | 2019-08-15 |
| 93 | 1026579088 | Norbey Bustamente | 7 | 30.6 | 1 | 2019-08-16 |
| 94 | 1026579088 | Norbey Bustamente | 56 | 34.8 | 2 | 2019-08-16 |
| 95 | 1026579088 | Norbey Bustamente | 5 | 19.2 | 3 | 2019-08-16 |
| 96 | 1026579088 | Norbey Bustamente | 5 | 18.6 | 4 | 2019-08-16 |
| 97 | 1026579088 | Norbey Bustamente | 20 | 49.8 | 5 | 2019-08-16 |
| 98 | 1026579088 | Norbey Bustamente | 13 | 51.6 | 6 | 2019-08-16 |
| 99 | 1026579088 | Norbey Bustamente | 39 | 60 | 7 | 2019-08-16 |
| 100 | 1026579088 | Norbey Bustamente | 9 | 49.8 | 8 | 2019-08-16 |
| 101 | 1026579088 | Norbey Bustamente | 20 | 96.6 | 9 | 2019-08-16 |
| 102 | 1026579088 | Norbey Bustamente | 139 | 352.2 | 10 | 2019-08-16 |

| ID | ident | name | Time | distance | level | date |
|---|---|---|---|---|---|---|
| 103 | 1026579088 | Norbey Bustamente | 67 | 299.4 | 11 | 2019-08-16 |
| 104 | 1026579088 | Norbey Bustamante | 127 | 316.8 | 12 | 2019-08-16 |
| 105 | 1026579088 | Norbey Bustamante | 23 | 97.8 | 13 | 2019-08-16 |
| 106 | 1026579088 | Norbey Bustamante | 129 | 121.8 | 14 | 2019-08-16 |
| 107 | 1026579088 | Norbey Bustamante | 6 | 30.6 | 1 | 2019-08-17 |
| 108 | 1026579088 | Norbey Bustamante | 7 | 30 | 2 | 2019-08-17 |
| 109 | 1026579088 | Norbey Bustamante | 4 | 19.2 | 3 | 2019-08-17 |
| 110 | 1026579088 | Norbey Bustamante | 4 | 18.6 | 4 | 2019-08-17 |
| 111 | 1026579088 | Norbey Bustamante | 9 | 49.8 | 5 | 2019-08-17 |
| ID | ident | name | Time | distance | level | date |
| 112 | 1026579088 | Norbey Bustamante | 8 | 50.4 | 6 | 2019-08-17 |
| 113 | 1026579088 | Norbey Bustamante | 8 | 49.2 | 7 | 2019-08-17 |
| 114 | 1026579088 | Norbey Bustamante | 8 | 49.8 | 8 | 2019-08-17 |
| 115 | 1026579088 | Norbey Bustamante | 23 | 96.6 | 9 | 2019-08-17 |

| ID | ident | name | Time | distance | level | date |
|---|---|---|---|---|---|---|
| 116 | 1026579088 | Norbey Bustamante | 59 | 263.4 | 10 | 2019-08-17 |
| 117 | 1026579088 | Norbey Bustamante | 65 | 298.8 | 11 | 2019-08-17 |
| 118 | 1026579088 | Norbey Bustamante | 73 | 315.6 | 12 | 2019-08-17 |
| 119 | 1026579088 | Norbey Bustamante | 31 | 97.8 | 13 | 2019-08-17 |
| 120 | 1026579088 | Norbey Bustamante | 37 | 106.2 | 14 | 2019-08-17 |
| 121 | 1026579088 | Norbey BUstamante | 37 | 35.4 | 1 | 2019-08-18 |
| 122 | 1026579088 | Norbey BUstamante | 8 | 30.6 | 2 | 2019-08-18 |
| 123 | 1026579088 | Norbey BUstamante | 26 | 20.4 | 3 | 2019-08-18 |
| 124 | 1026579088 | Norbey BUstamante | 7 | 18.6 | 4 | 2019-08-18 |
| 125 | 1026579088 | Norbey BUstamante | 133 | 168 | 5 | 2019-08-18 |
| 126 | 1026579088 | Norbey BUstamante | 7 | 50.4 | 6 | 2019-08-18 |
| 127 | 1026579088 | Norbey BUstamante | 69 | 51.6 | 7 | 2019-08-18 |
| 128 | 1026579088 | Norbey BUstamante | 12 | 76.2 | 8 | 2019-08-18 |
| 129 | 1026579088 | Norbey BUstamante | 27 | 128.4 | 9 | 2019-08-18 |

| ID | ident | name | Time | distance | level | date |
| --- | --- | --- | --- | --- | --- | --- |
| 130 | 1026579088 | Norbey BUstamante | 112 | 297.6 | 10 | 2019-08-18 |
| 131 | 1026579088 | Norbey BUstamante | 88 | 299.4 | 11 | 2019-08-18 |
| 132 | 1026579088 | Norbey BUstamante | 171 | 384.6 | 12 | 2019-08-18 |
| 133 | 1026579088 | Norbey BUstamante | 16 | 97.8 | 13 | 2019-08-18 |
| 134 | 1026579088 | Norbey BUstamante | 76 | 157.8 | 14 | 2019-08-18 |

# Appendix C: Multilevel Development

In this Annex the Multilevels developed for the treatment of JTS and FDR are shown. These Multilevels are a total of 14, and will be identified with the subtitle "Level x", where x will correspond to the level of difficulty.

**Level 1**

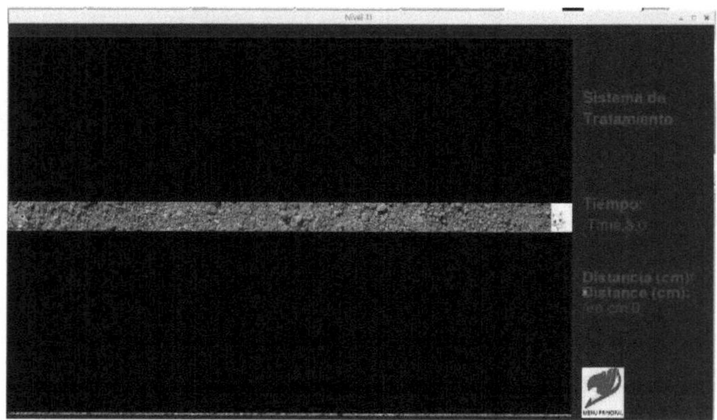

**Level 2**

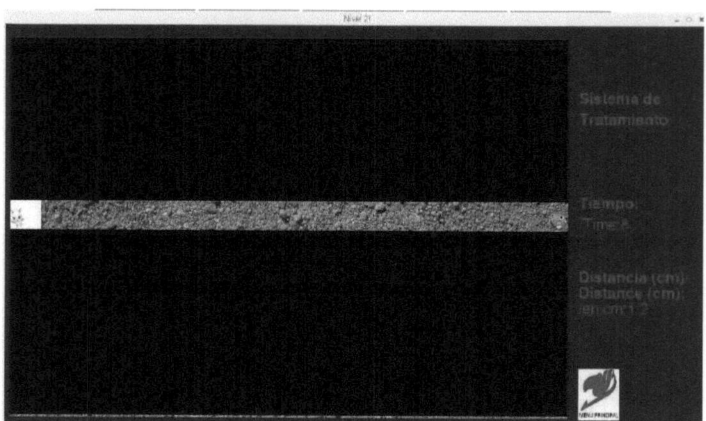

## Level 3

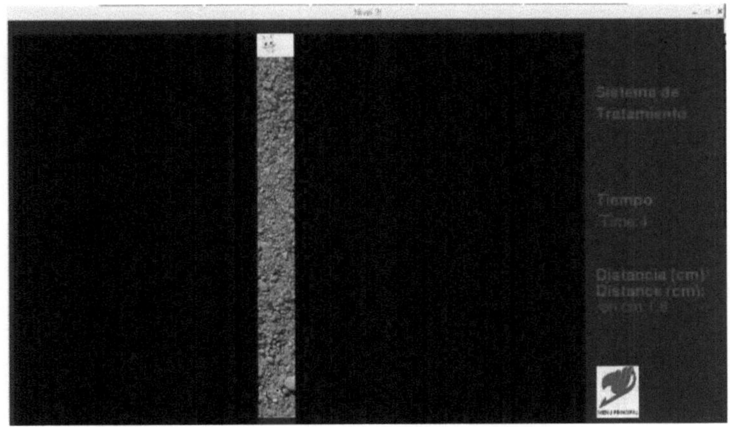

## Level 4

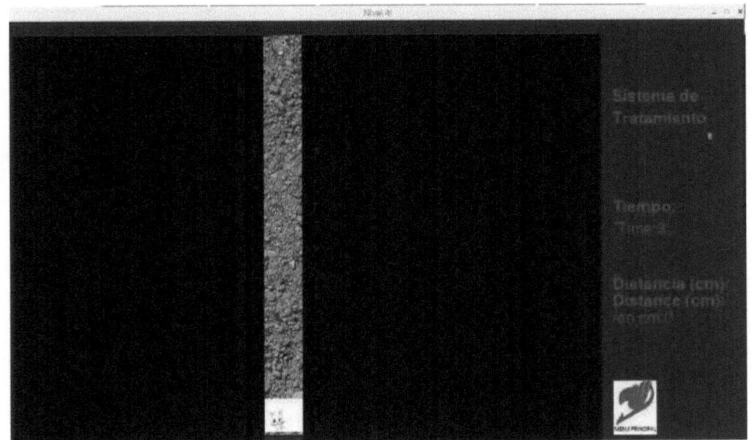

# Level 5

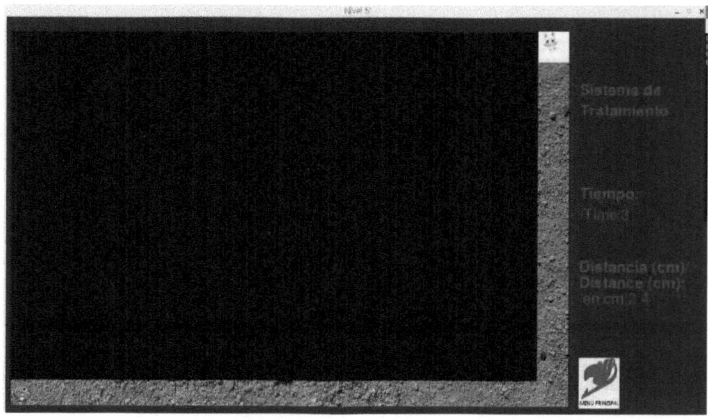

# Level 6

## Level 7

## Level 8

# Level 9

# Level 10

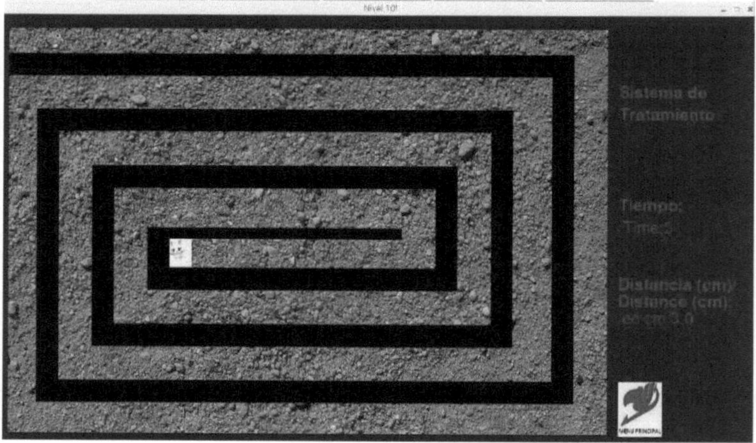

# Level 11

# Level 12

# Level 13

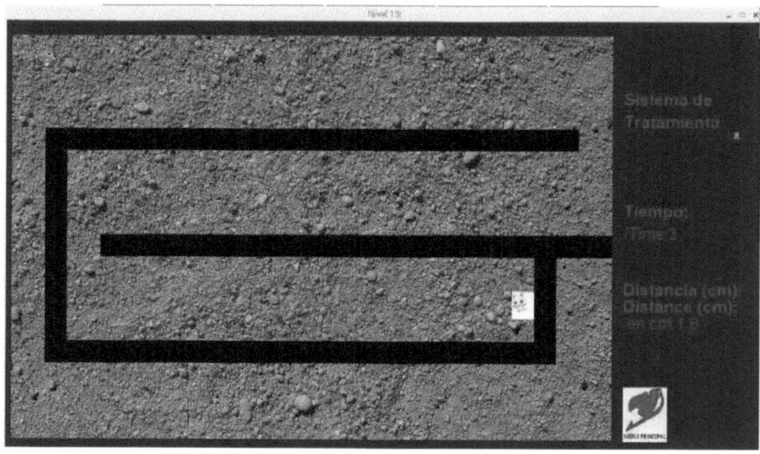

# Level 14

# Bibliography


[1]   Grupo Sura, "blog.segurossura.com.co," 15 April 2012. [On line]. Available: https://blog.segurossura.com.co/articulo/salud/tunel-carpiano. [Last access: 08 September 2019].

[2]   J. Pastor, "Xataca," February 22, 2018 [On line]. Available: https://www.xataka.com/medicina-y-salud/el-sindrome-del-tunel-carpiano-como-enfermedad-profesional-ahora-tambien-afecta-al-comercio. [Last access: 08 September 2019].

[3]   OrthoInfo, "https://orthoinfo.aaos.org," January 2014. Online]. Available: https://orthoinfo.aaos.org/es/diseases--conditions/fracturas-distales-del-radio-muneca-quebrada-distal-radius-fractures/. [Last accessed: 08 September 2019].

[4]   H. R. D. v. d. H. A. v. T. R. B. D. A. R. B. L. Sofia Ramiro, "Cochrane," October 05, 2011. Online]. Available: https://www.cochrane.org/es/CD008886/tratamiento-combinado-para-el-control-del-dolor-en-la-artritis-inflamatoria-artritis-reumatoide. [Last accessed: September 08, 2019].

[5]   Igenomix, "nace.igenomix.es,' September 26, 2018. [On line]. Available: https://nace.igenomix.es/blog/sindrome-del-tunel-carpiano-en-el-embarazo-que-es-y-como-aliviarlo/. [Last access: 08 September 2019].

[6]   UN News Agency, "Unimedios - Agencia de Noticias UN," May 21, 2018. [On line]. Available: https://agenciadenoticias.unal.edu.co/detalle/article/dispositivo-ayudaria-a-prevenir-cirugia-de-tunel-carpiano.html. [Last access: 08 September 2019].

[7]   A. M. L. Azcona, "OrtoWeb," OrtoWeb.com, 25 September 2018. [On line]. Available: http://www.ortoweb.com/blogortopedia/munequeras-para-el-sindrome-del-tunel-carpiano/. [Last accessed: 08 September 2019].

[8]   A. F. G. E. G. Gabriela Cristina García Parra, "Carpal Tunnel Syndrome," Morfolia Year 1 - Vol. 3, Bogota D.C., 2009.

[9]   D. F. B. Borrero, "Las Fracturas del Antebrazo en el Adulto y el Compromiso de los Elementos Ligamentaros Asociados a Ellas," *Revista Colombiana de Ortopedia y Traumatología,* vol. 11, no. 2, p. Orthopedia, 1997.

[10] M. L. PAREJA, "vitonica.com," December 12, 2014 [On line]. Available: https://www.vitonica.com/fisioterapia/cuantas-sesiones-de-fisioterapia-son-necesarias-para-recuperase-de-una-lesion. [Last access: 08 September 2019].

[11] M. Foord, "python.org," 04 June 2019. Online]. Available: https://docs.python.org/2/howto/urllib2.html. Last access: 08 September 2019.

[12] DBA Dixit, "http://dbadixit.com," 01 December 2017. Online]. Available: http://dbadixit.com/llave-primaria-primary-key-una-tabla/. [Last access: 08 September 2019].

[13] matplotlib.org, "matplotlib.org," August 26, 2019. [Online]. Available: https://matplotlib.org. [Last access: 08 September 2019].

[14] http://mercurio.ugr.es, "http://mercurio.ugr.es," [Online]. Available: http://mercurio.ugr.es/pedro/tutoriales/php/php.html. [Last access: 08 September 2019].

[15] C. Villagómez, "The HTTP Protocol," CCM, 17 January 2018. Online]. Available: https://es.ccm.net/contents/264-el-protocolo-http. [Last access: 08 September 2019].

[16] C. Villagómez, "es.kioskea.net," 17 January 2018. Online]. Available: https://es.ccm.net/contents/264-el-protocolo-http. [Last access: 08 September 2019].

[17] twilio, "twilio Docs," [Online]. Available: https://www.twilio.com/docs/api. [Last access: 08 September 2019].

[18] REDACCION EL TIEMPO, "El Tiempo.com," El Tiempo, 04 April 2005. [On line]. Available: https://www.eltiempo.com/archivo/documento/MAM-1623544. [Last access: 08 September 2019].